Water Everywhere

PIG RESCUE!

By James Buckley Jr.

Illustrated by Kerstin LaCross

BEARPORT
PUBLISHING

Minneapolis, Minnesota

BEAR
CLAW

Credits

Interior coloring by Jon Siruno.
Photos: 22T © Mike Simons/Tulsa World/AP Photos; 22B © Felipe Dana/AP Photos.

Bearport Publishing
Minneapolis, MN
President: Jen Jenson
Director of Product Development: Spencer Brinker
Editor: Allison Juda

Produced by Shoreline Publishing Group LLC
Santa Barbara, California
Designer: Patty Kelley
Editorial Director: James Buckley Jr.

DISCLAIMER: This graphic story is a dramatization based on true events. It is intended to give the reader a sense of the narrative rather than a presentation of actual details as they occurred.

Library of Congress Cataloging-in-Publication Data

Names: Buckley, James, Jr., 1963- author. | LaCross, Kerstin, 1988-
   illustrator.
Title: Water everywhere : pig rescue! / by James Buckley Jr. ; illustrated
   by Kerstin LaCross.
Description: Bear claw books [edition]. | Minneapolis, MN : Bearport
   Publishing Company, [2021] | Series: Rescued! animal escapes | Includes
   bibliographical references and index.
Identifiers: LCCN 2020035424 (print) | LCCN 2020035425 (ebook) | ISBN
   9781647476212 (library binding) | ISBN 9781647476281 (paperback) | ISBN
   9781647476359 (ebook)
Subjects: LCSH: Floods—Juvenile literature. | Swine—Juvenile literature.
Classification: LCC GB1399 .B774 2021 (print) | LCC GB1399 (ebook) | DDC
   363.34/93—dc23
LC record available at https://lccn.loc.gov/2020035424
LC ebook record available at https://lccn.loc.gov/2020035425

For more information, write to Bearport Publishing, 5357 Penn Avenue South, Minneapolis, MN 55419. Printed in the United States of America.

Contents

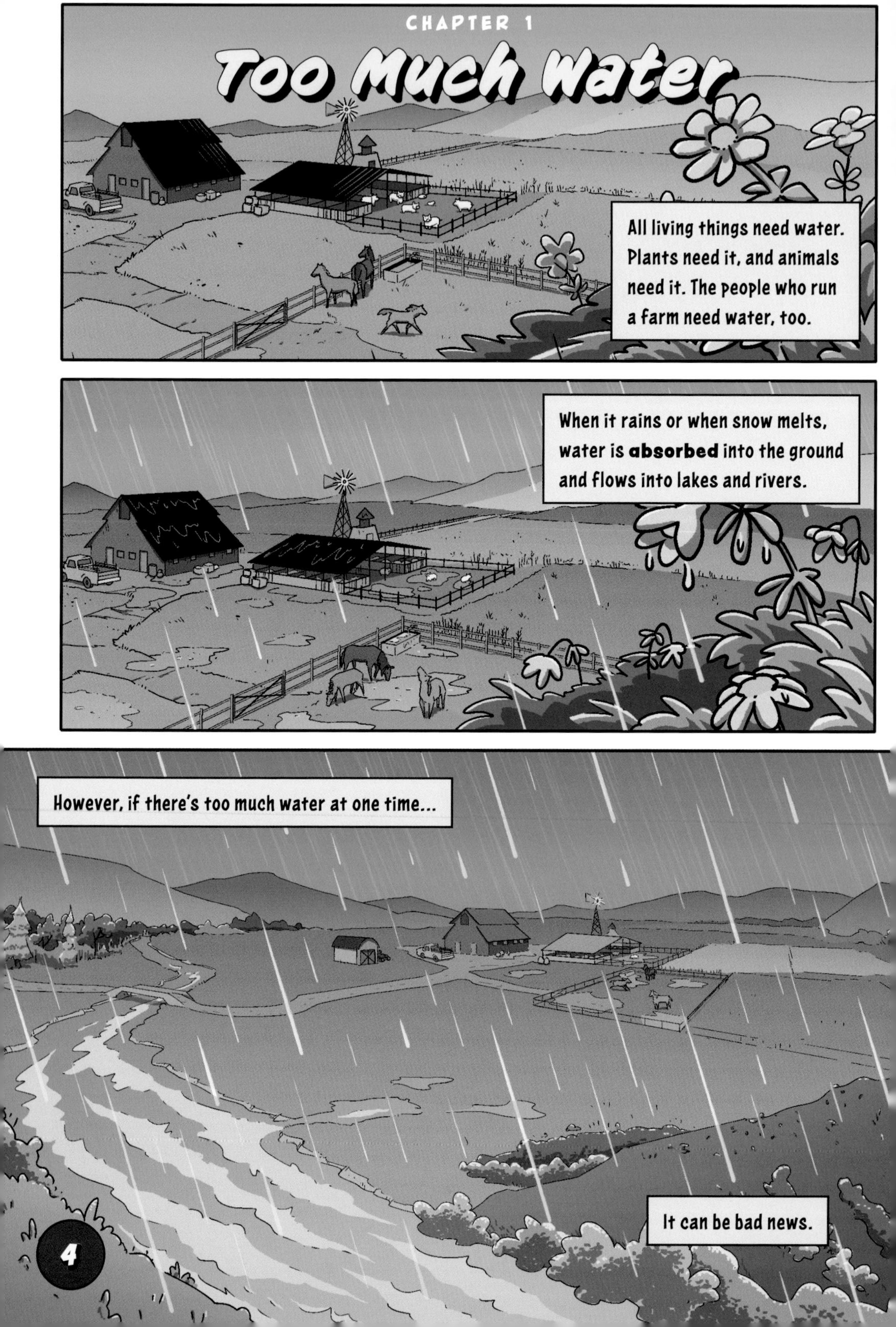
CHAPTER 1
Too Much Water
All living things need water. Plants need it, and animals need it. The people who run a farm need water, too.
When it rains or when snow melts, water is **absorbed** into the ground and flows into lakes and rivers.
However, if there's too much water at one time...
It can be bad news.

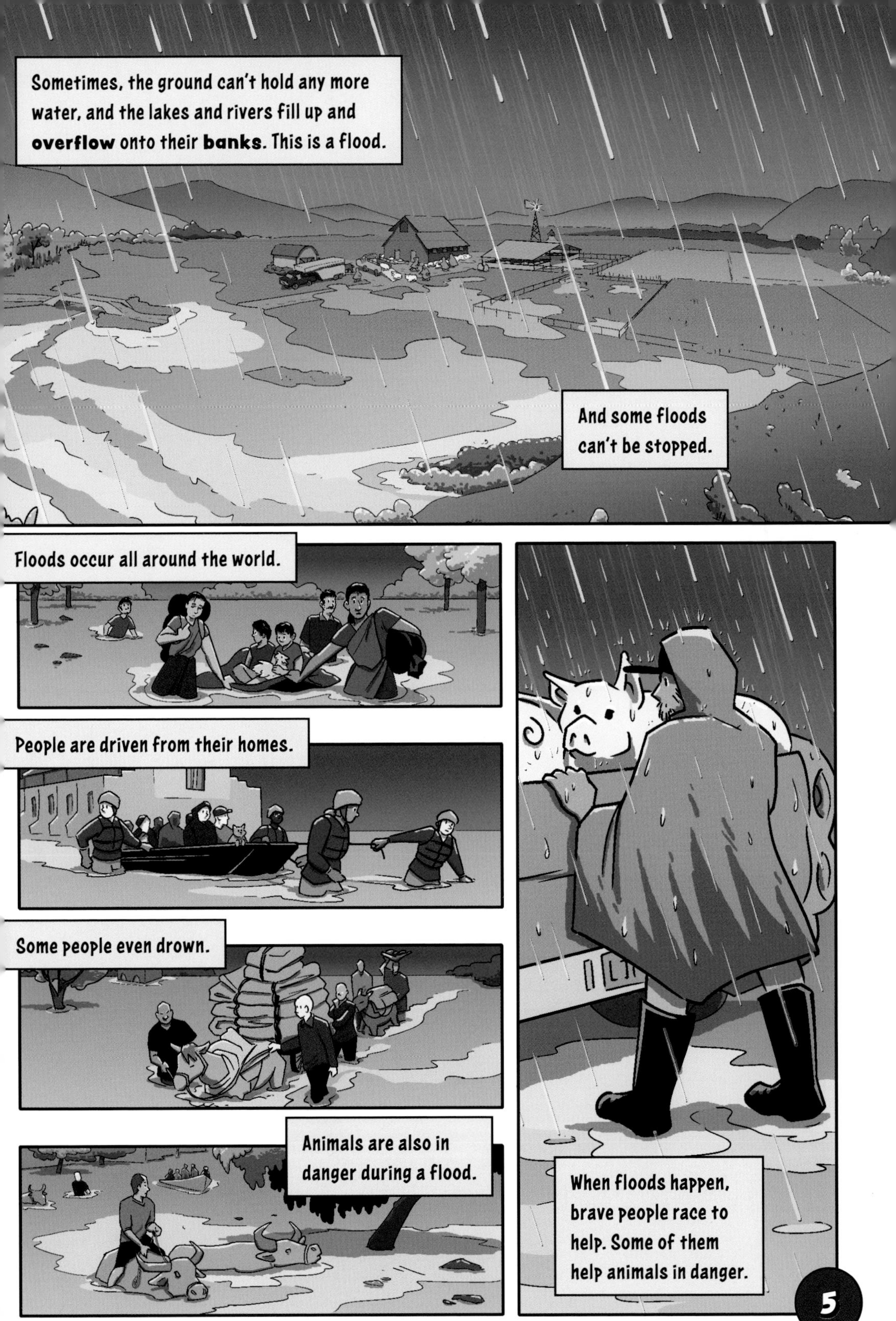
Sometimes, the ground can't hold any more water, and the lakes and rivers fill up and **overflow** onto their **banks**. This is a flood.
And some floods can't be stopped.
Floods occur all around the world.
People are driven from their homes.
Some people even drown.
Animals are also in danger during a flood.
When floods happen, brave people race to help. Some of them help animals in danger.

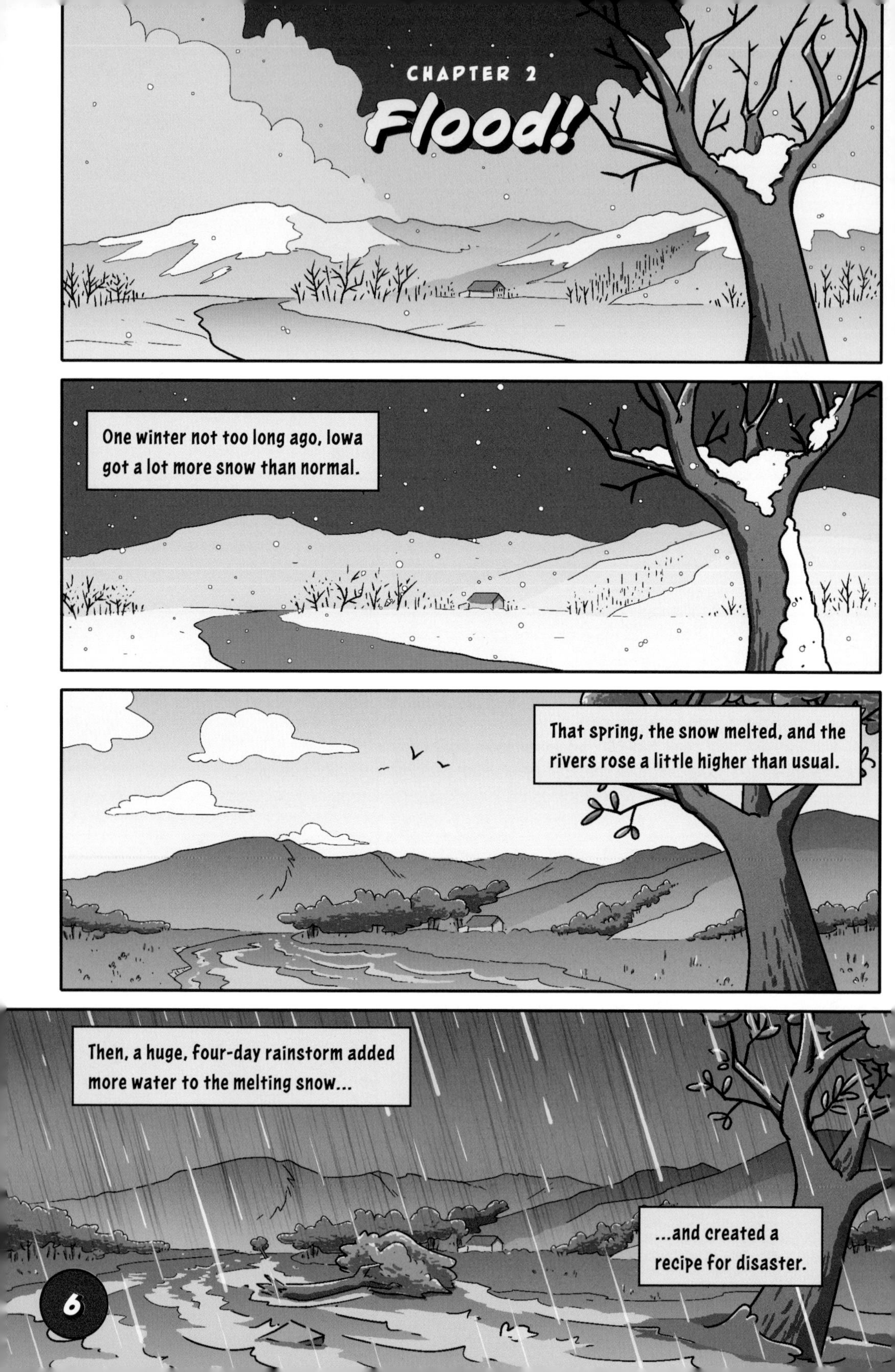
CHAPTER 2
Flood!
One winter not too long ago, Iowa got a lot more snow than normal.
That spring, the snow melted, and the rivers rose a little higher than usual.
Then, a huge, four-day rainstorm added more water to the melting snow...
...and created a recipe for disaster.

Jeff Johnson's Iowa pig farm was in the path of a flood.

LET'S PUT THE HORSES INSIDE!

I CAN'T BELIEVE ALL THIS RAIN. WILL IT EVER STOP?

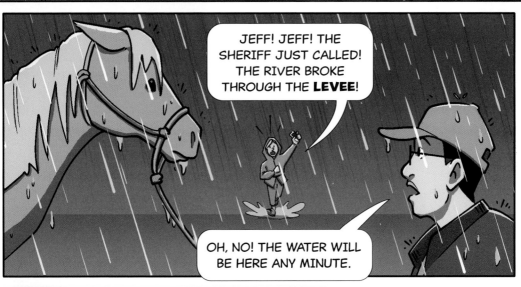

JEFF! JEFF! THE SHERIFF JUST CALLED! THE RIVER BROKE THROUGH THE **LEVEE**!

OH, NO! THE WATER WILL BE HERE ANY MINUTE.

WE GOTTA OPEN UP THE PIG PENS!

PIGS CAN SWIM, BUT THIS MIGHT BE TOO MUCH WATER FOR THEM!

7

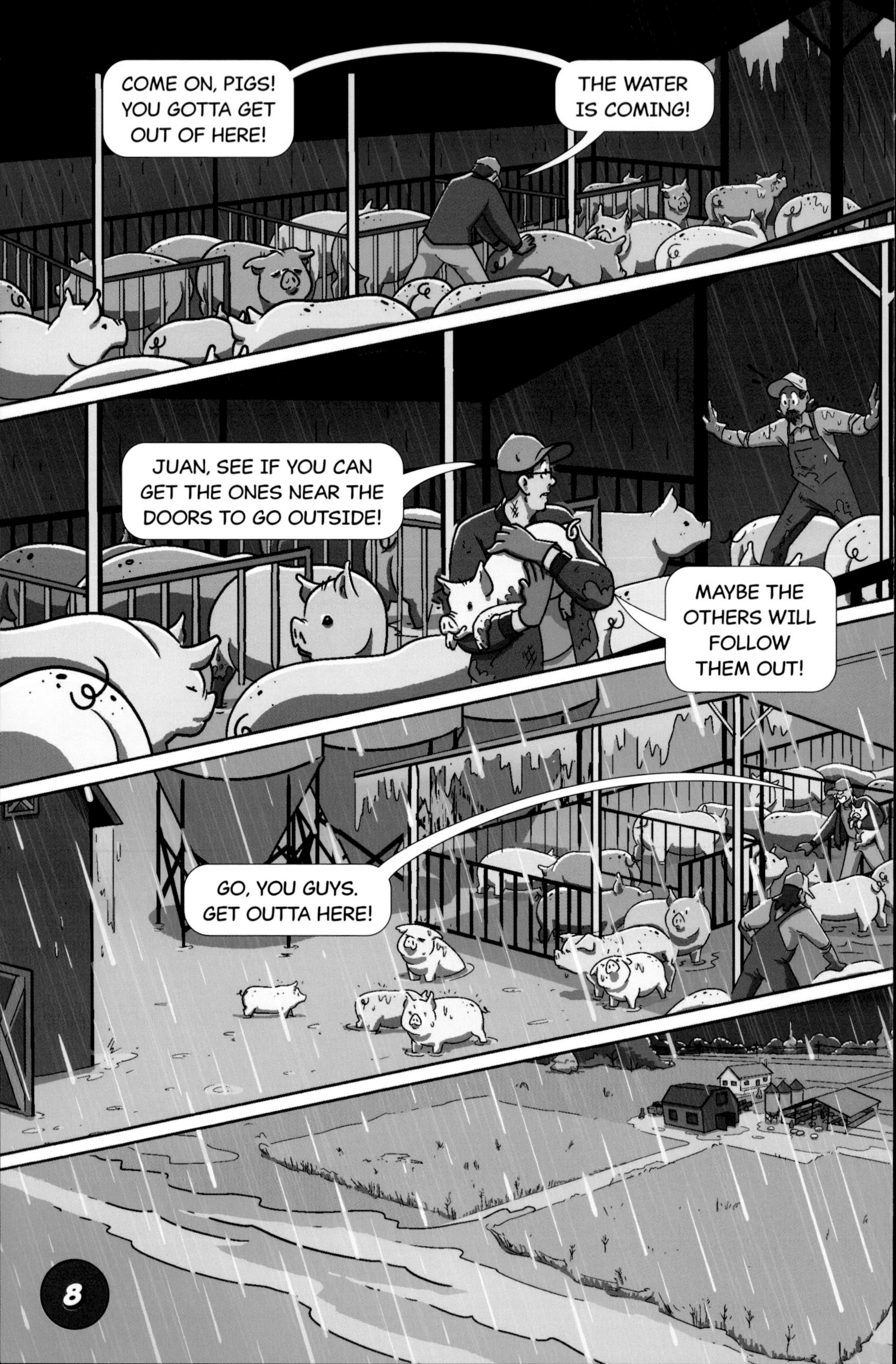
COME ON, PIGS! YOU GOTTA GET OUT OF HERE!
THE WATER IS COMING!
JUAN, SEE IF YOU CAN GET THE ONES NEAR THE DOORS TO GO OUTSIDE!
MAYBE THE OTHERS WILL FOLLOW THEM OUT!
GO, YOU GUYS. GET OUTTA HERE!

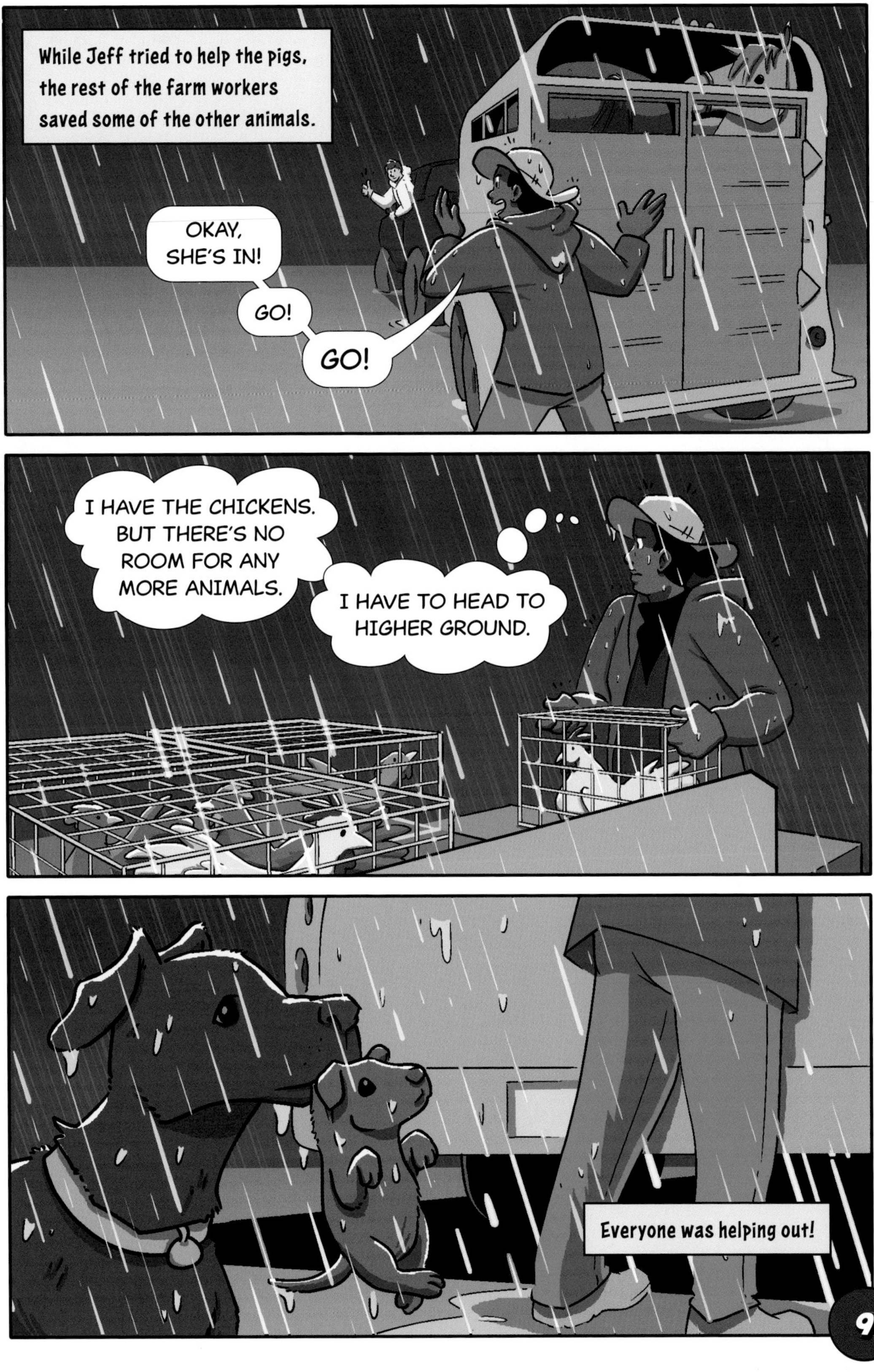
While Jeff tried to help the pigs, the rest of the farm workers saved some of the other animals.
OKAY, SHE'S IN!
GO!
GO!
I HAVE THE CHICKENS. BUT THERE'S NO ROOM FOR ANY MORE ANIMALS.
I HAVE TO HEAD TO HIGHER GROUND.
Everyone was helping out!

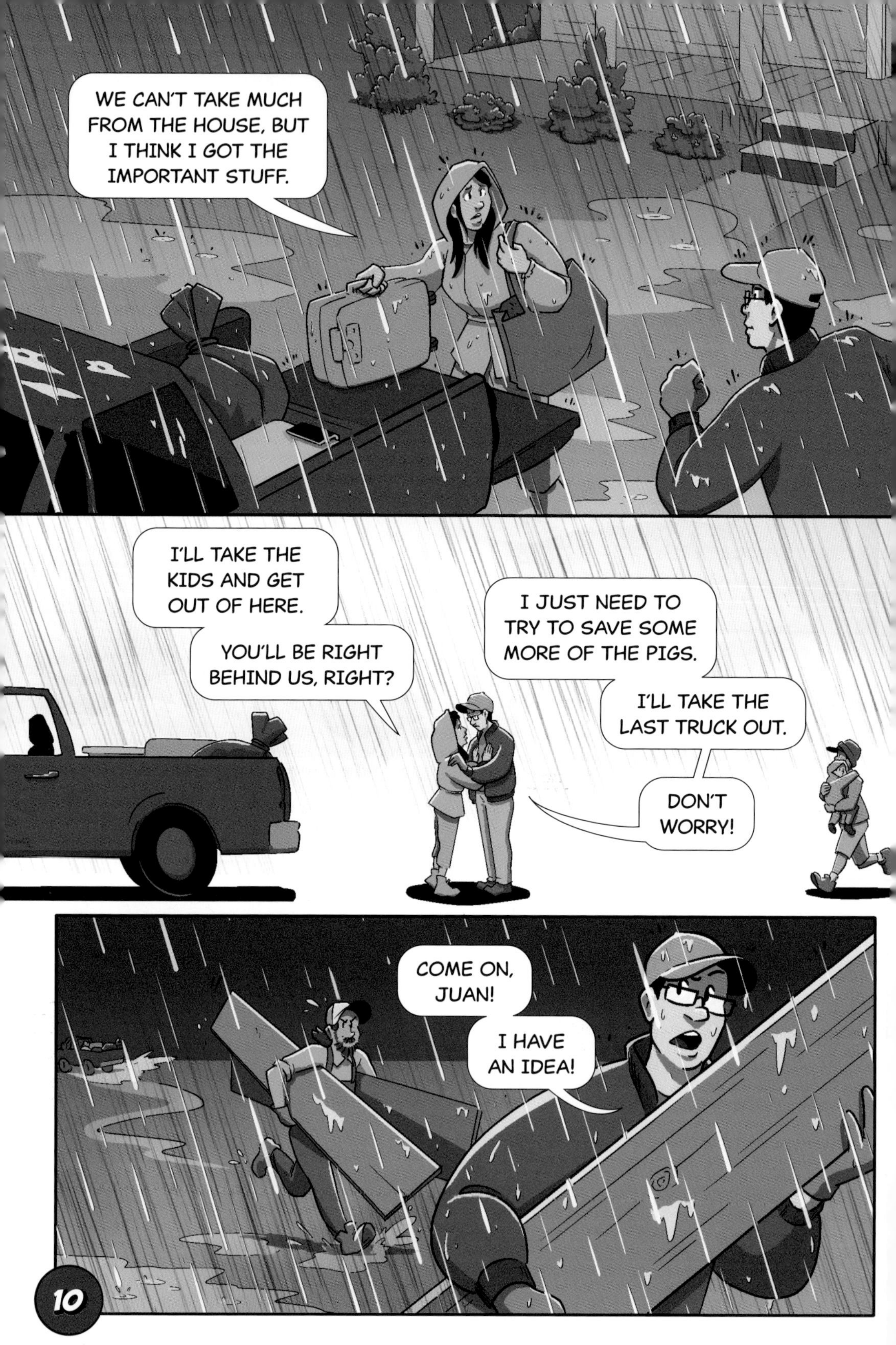

WE CAN'T TAKE MUCH FROM THE HOUSE, BUT I THINK I GOT THE IMPORTANT STUFF.
I'LL TAKE THE KIDS AND GET OUT OF HERE.
YOU'LL BE RIGHT BEHIND US, RIGHT?
I JUST NEED TO TRY TO SAVE SOME MORE OF THE PIGS.
I'LL TAKE THE LAST TRUCK OUT.
DON'T WORRY!
COME ON, JUAN!
I HAVE AN IDEA!

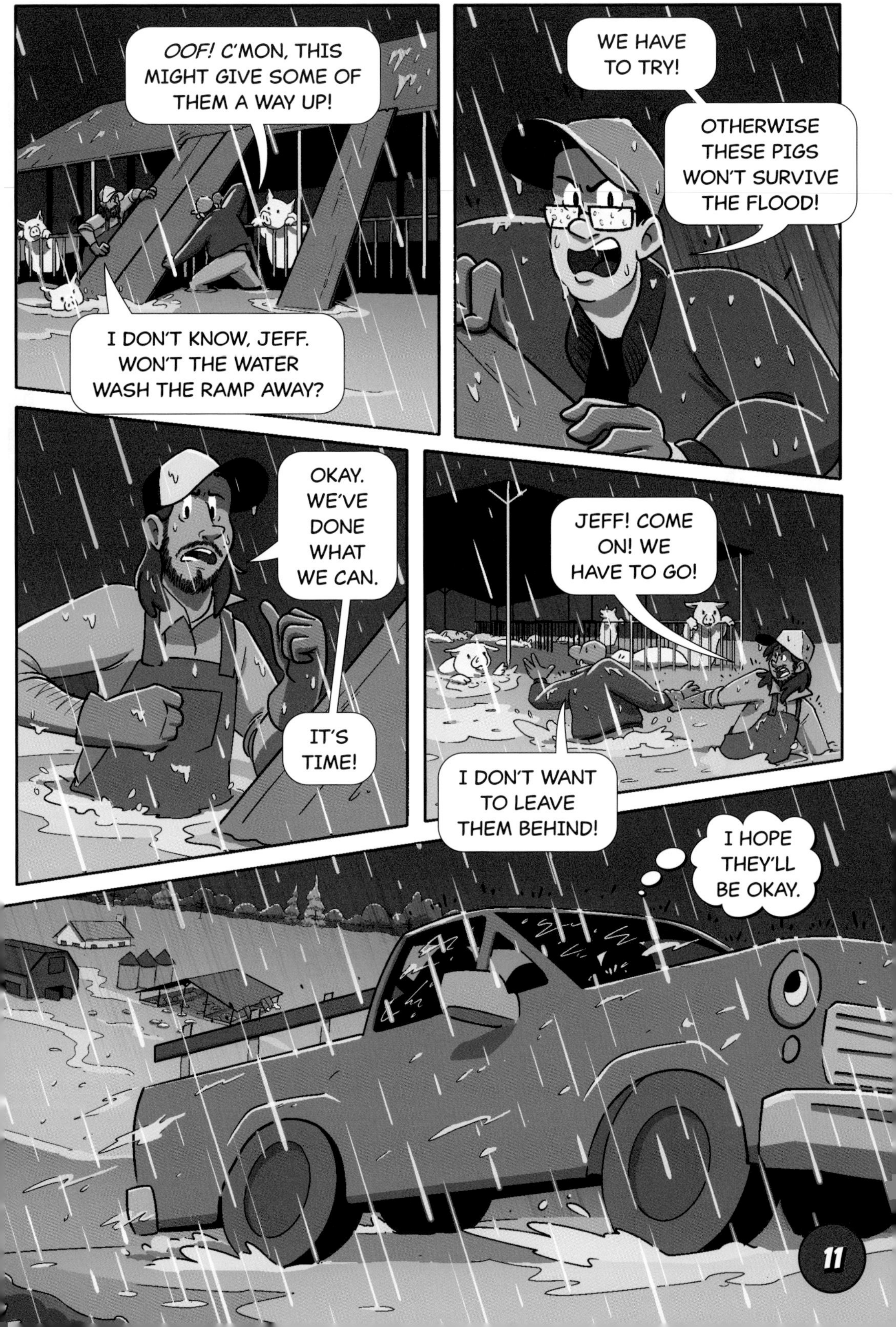
OOF! C'MON, THIS MIGHT GIVE SOME OF THEM A WAY UP!
I DON'T KNOW, JEFF. WON'T THE WATER WASH THE RAMP AWAY?
WE HAVE TO TRY!
OTHERWISE THESE PIGS WON'T SURVIVE THE FLOOD!
OKAY. WE'VE DONE WHAT WE CAN.
IT'S TIME!
JEFF! COME ON! WE HAVE TO GO!
I DON'T WANT TO LEAVE THEM BEHIND!
I HOPE THEY'LL BE OKAY.

CHAPTER 3

Little Pink Dots

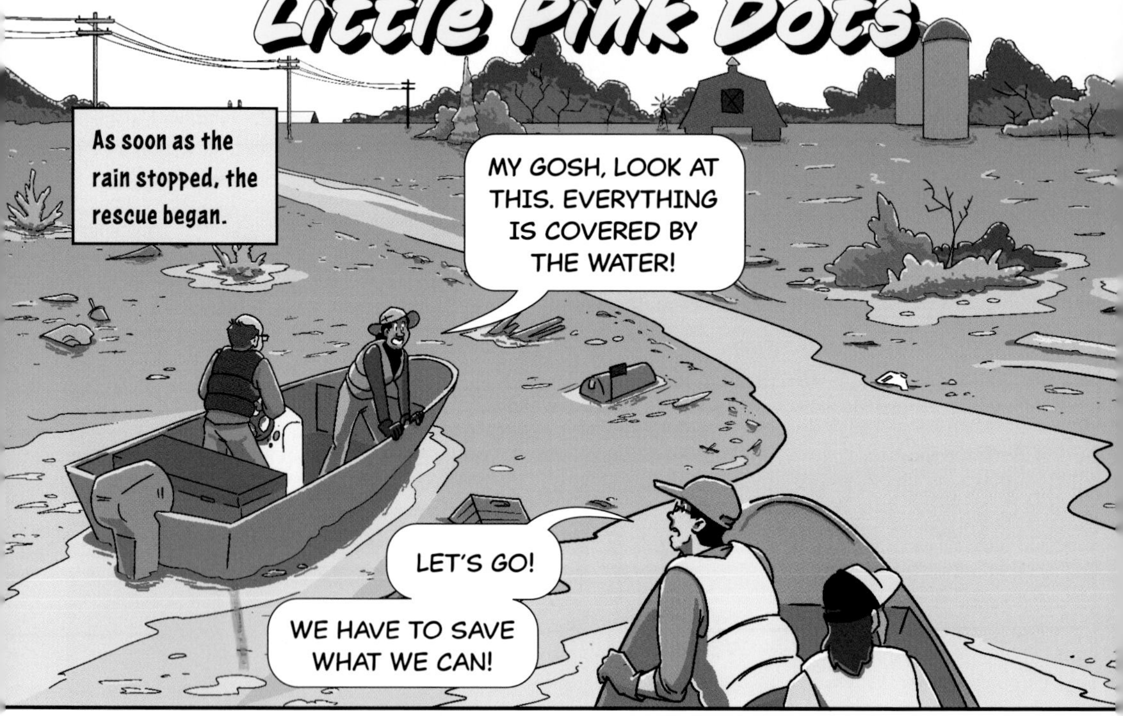
As soon as the rain stopped, the rescue began.
MY GOSH, LOOK AT THIS. EVERYTHING IS COVERED BY THE WATER!
LET'S GO!
WE HAVE TO SAVE WHAT WE CAN!

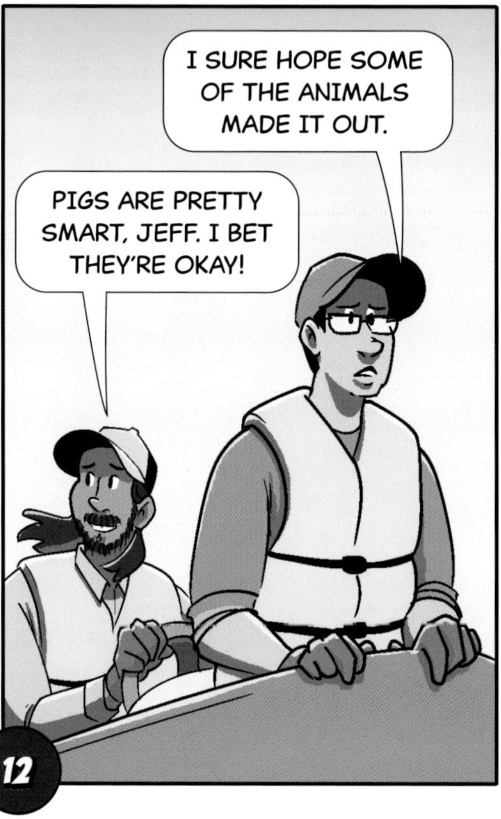
I SURE HOPE SOME OF THE ANIMALS MADE IT OUT.
PIGS ARE PRETTY SMART, JEFF. I BET THEY'RE OKAY!

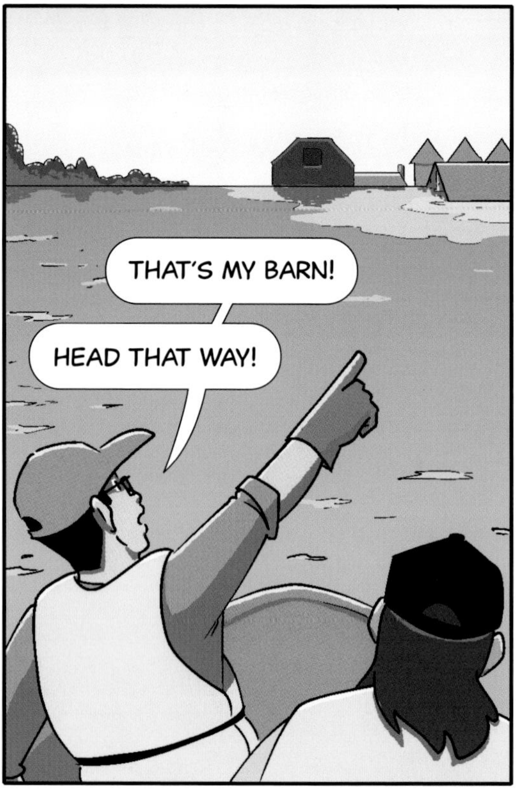
THAT'S MY BARN!
HEAD THAT WAY!

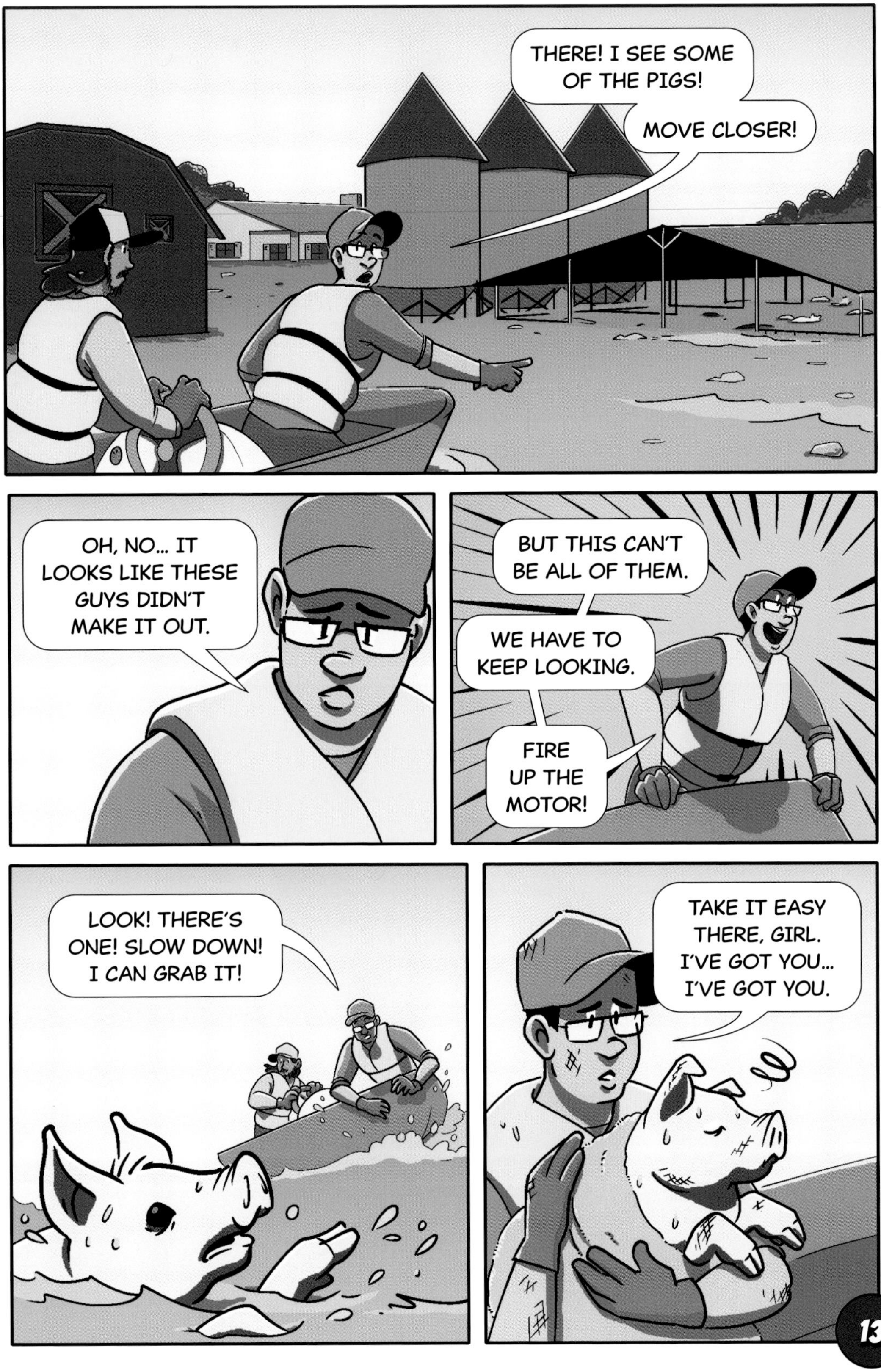
THERE! I SEE SOME OF THE PIGS!
MOVE CLOSER!
OH, NO... IT LOOKS LIKE THESE GUYS DIDN'T MAKE IT OUT.
BUT THIS CAN'T BE ALL OF THEM.
WE HAVE TO KEEP LOOKING.
FIRE UP THE MOTOR!
LOOK! THERE'S ONE! SLOW DOWN! I CAN GRAB IT!
TAKE IT EASY THERE, GIRL. I'VE GOT YOU... I'VE GOT YOU.

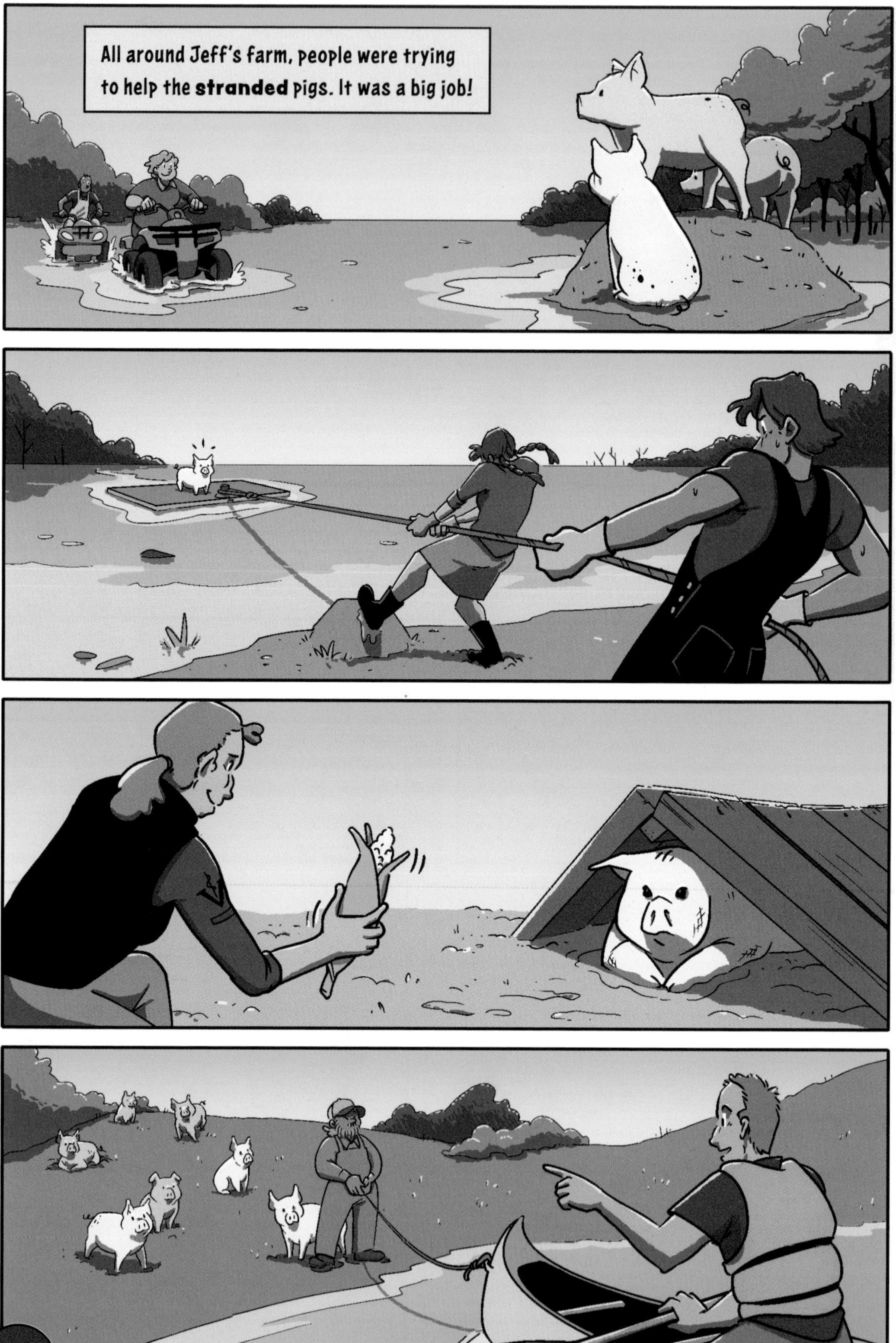
All around Jeff's farm, people were trying to help the **stranded** pigs. It was a big job!

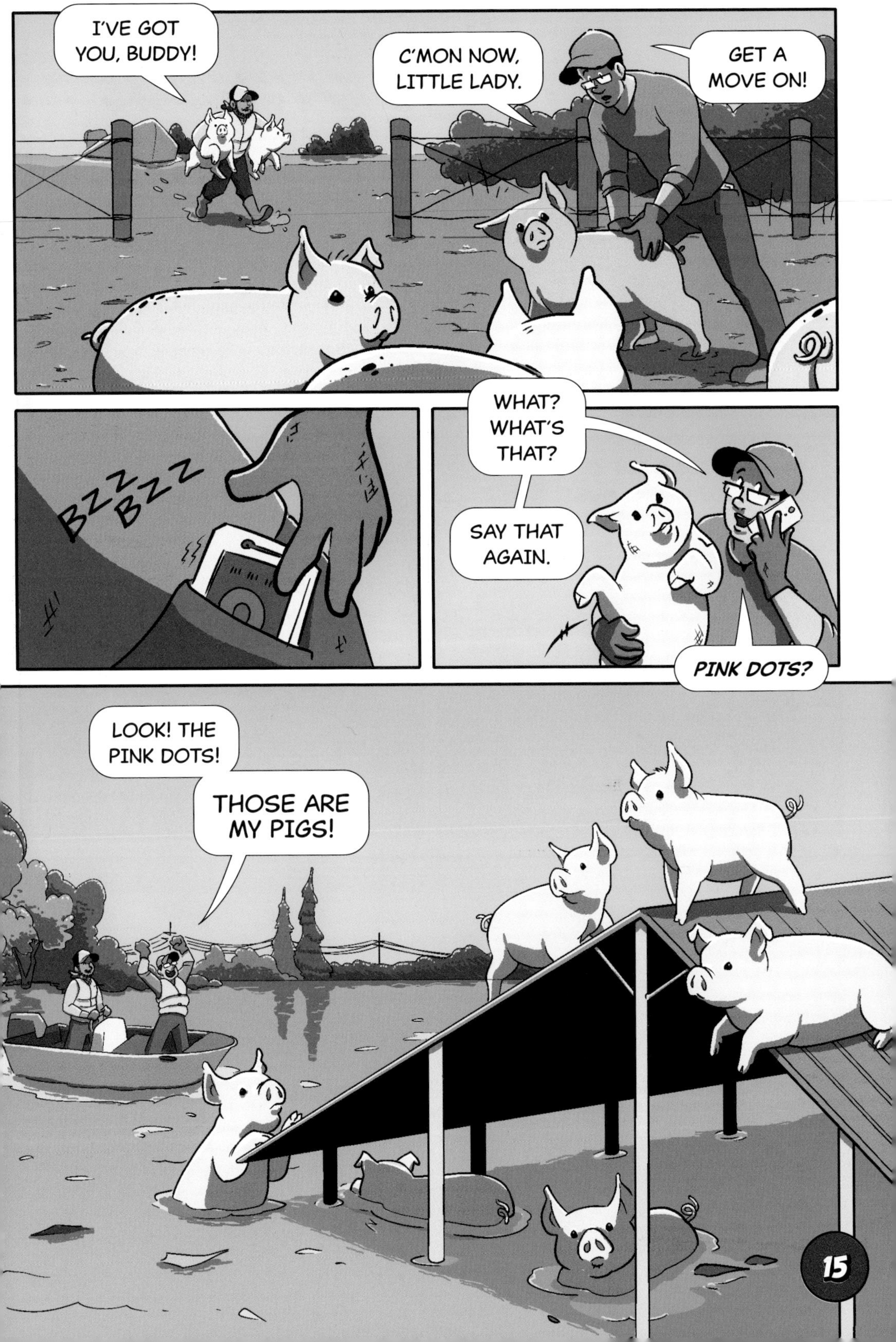
I'VE GOT YOU, BUDDY!
C'MON NOW, LITTLE LADY.
GET A MOVE ON!
BZZ BZZ
WHAT? WHAT'S THAT?
SAY THAT AGAIN.
PINK DOTS?
LOOK! THE PINK DOTS!
THOSE ARE MY PIGS!

CHAPTER 4

Soggy Pigs Dry Out

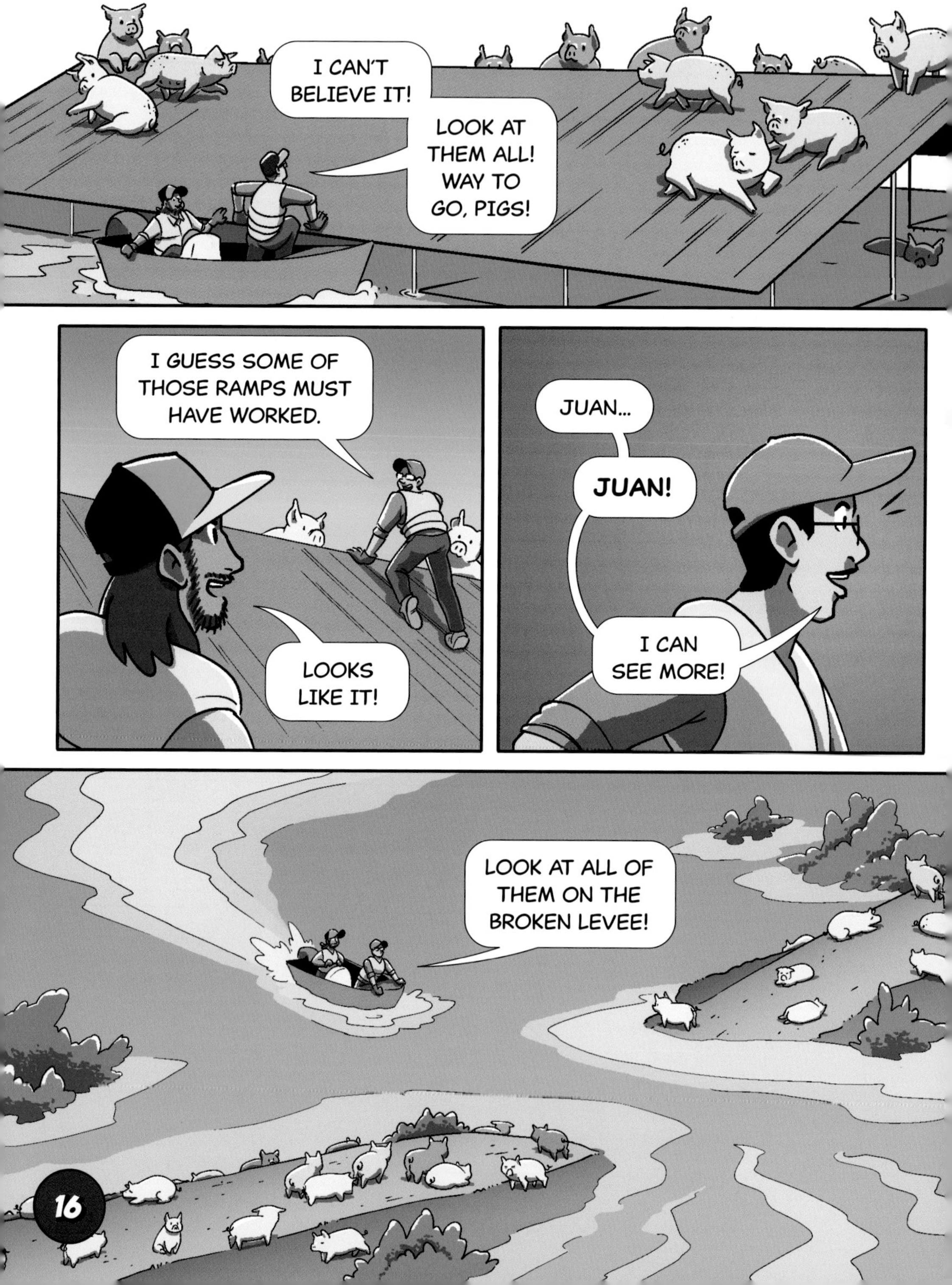
I CAN'T BELIEVE IT!
LOOK AT THEM ALL! WAY TO GO, PIGS!
I GUESS SOME OF THOSE RAMPS MUST HAVE WORKED.
LOOKS LIKE IT!
JUAN...
JUAN!
I CAN SEE MORE!
LOOK AT ALL OF THEM ON THE BROKEN LEVEE!

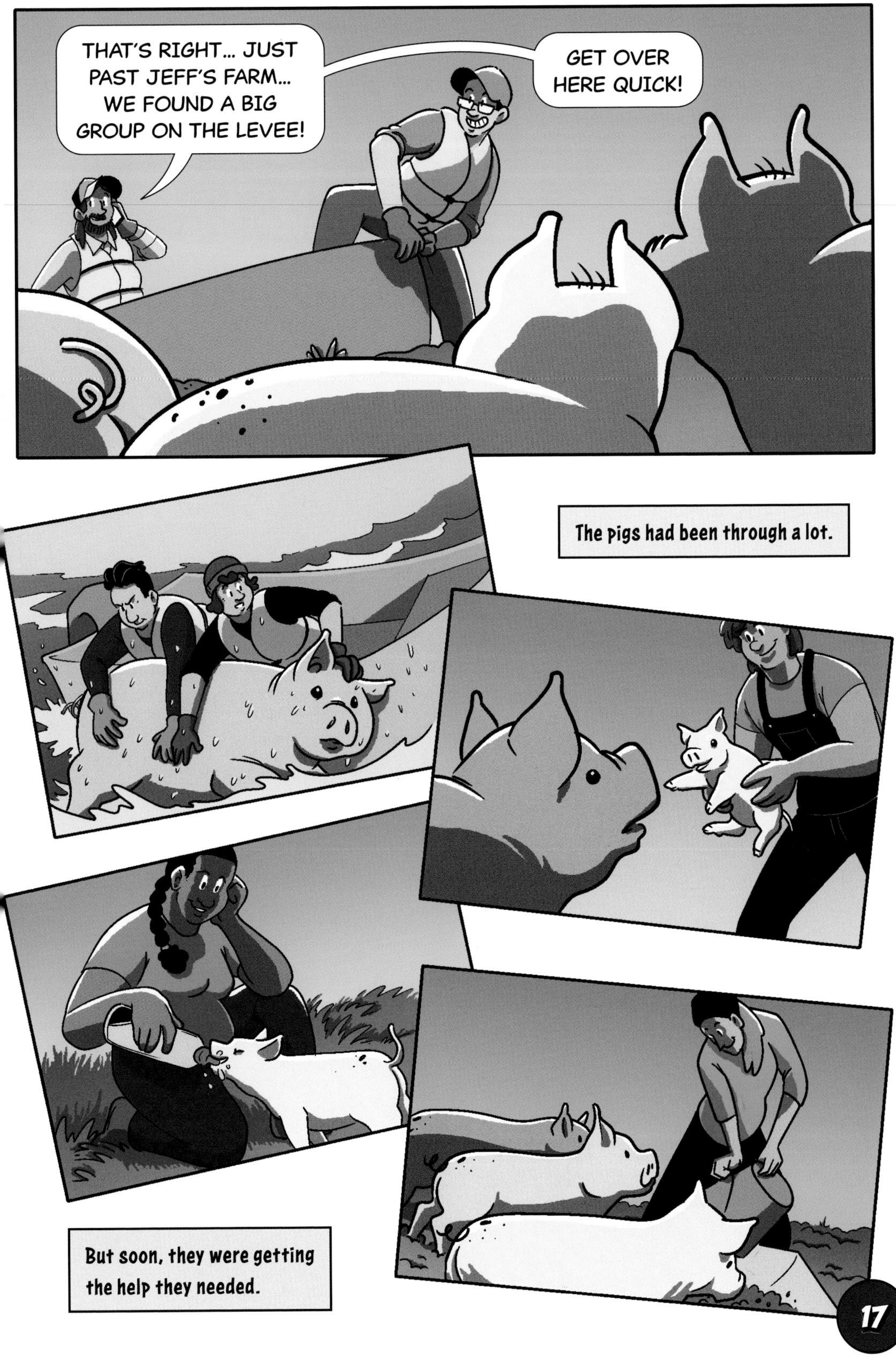
THAT'S RIGHT... JUST PAST JEFF'S FARM... WE FOUND A BIG GROUP ON THE LEVEE!
GET OVER HERE QUICK!
The pigs had been through a lot.
But soon, they were getting the help they needed.

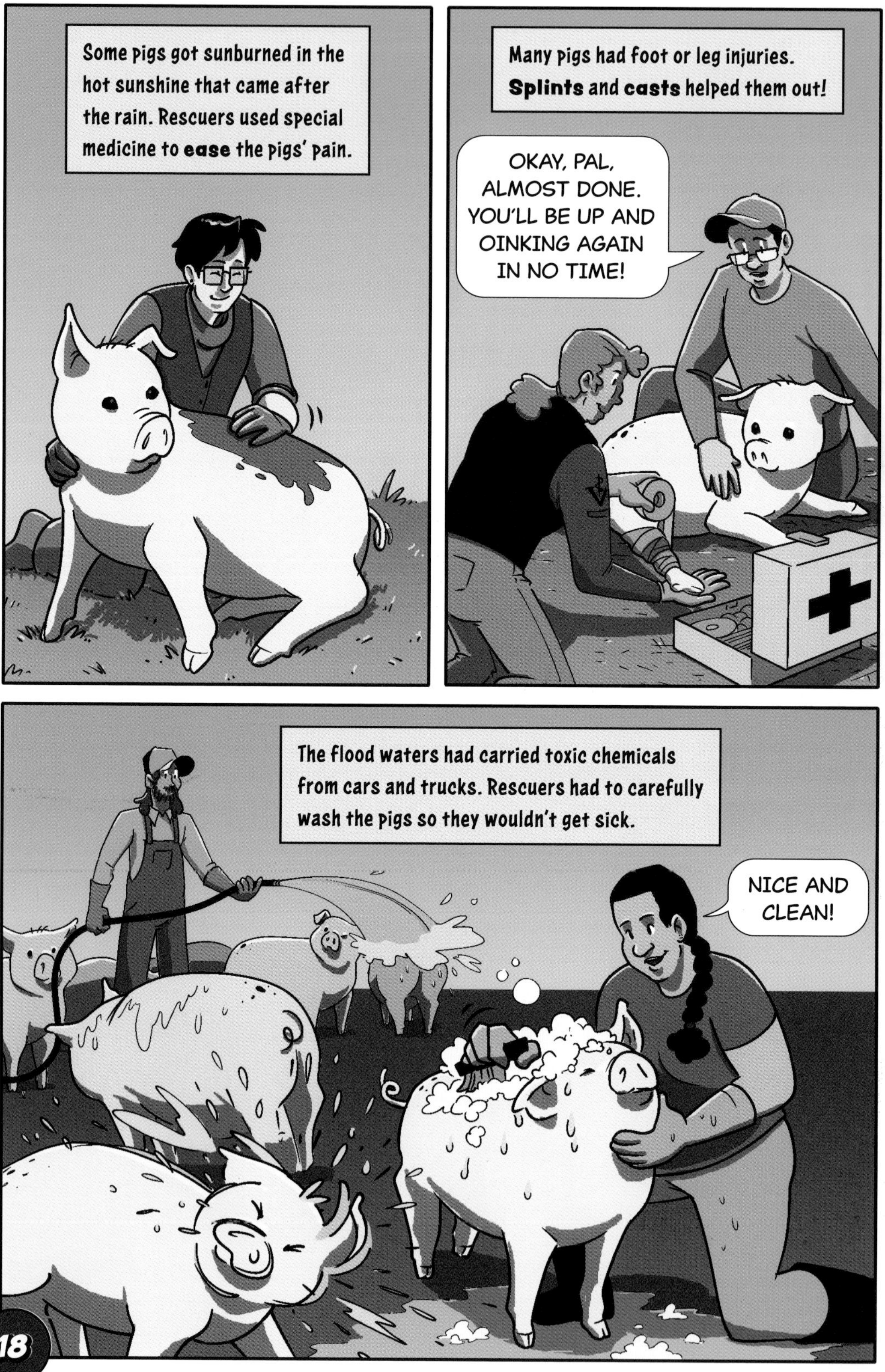
Some pigs got sunburned in the hot sunshine that came after the rain. Rescuers used special medicine to ease the pigs' pain.
Many pigs had foot or leg injuries. Splints and casts helped them out!
OKAY, PAL, ALMOST DONE. YOU'LL BE UP AND OINKING AGAIN IN NO TIME!
The flood waters had carried toxic chemicals from cars and trucks. Rescuers had to carefully wash the pigs so they wouldn't get sick.
NICE AND CLEAN!

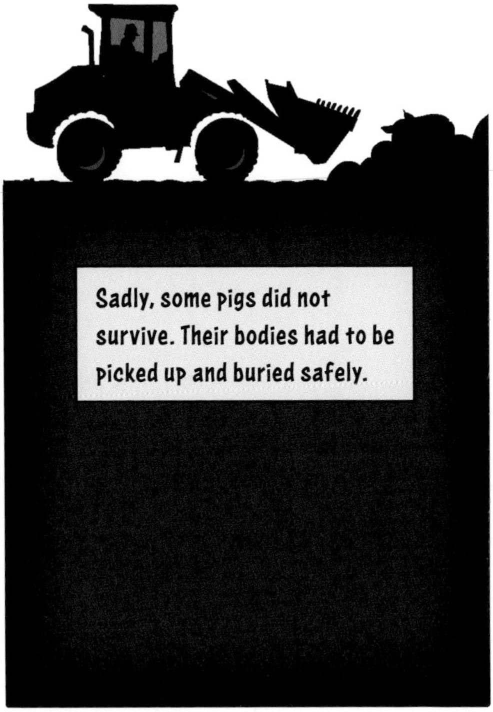
Sadly, some pigs did not survive. Their bodies had to be picked up and buried safely.

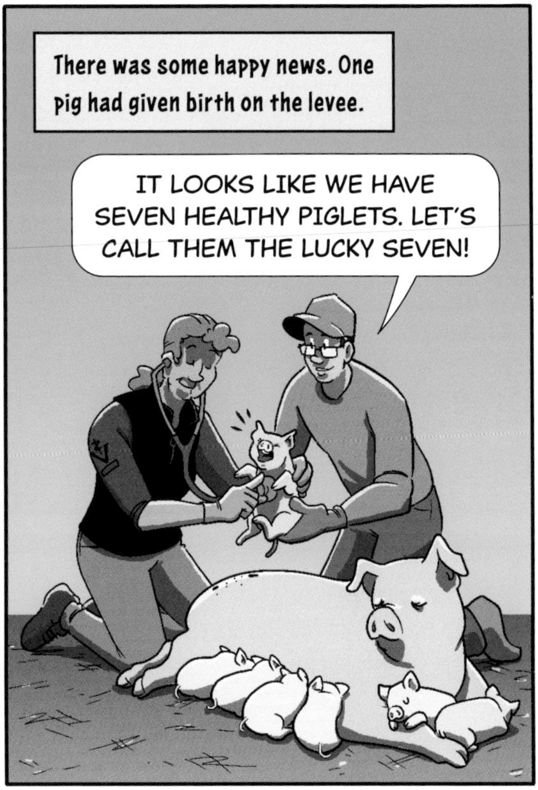
There was some happy news. One pig had given birth on the levee.
IT LOOKS LIKE WE HAVE SEVEN HEALTHY PIGLETS. LET'S CALL THEM THE LUCKY SEVEN!

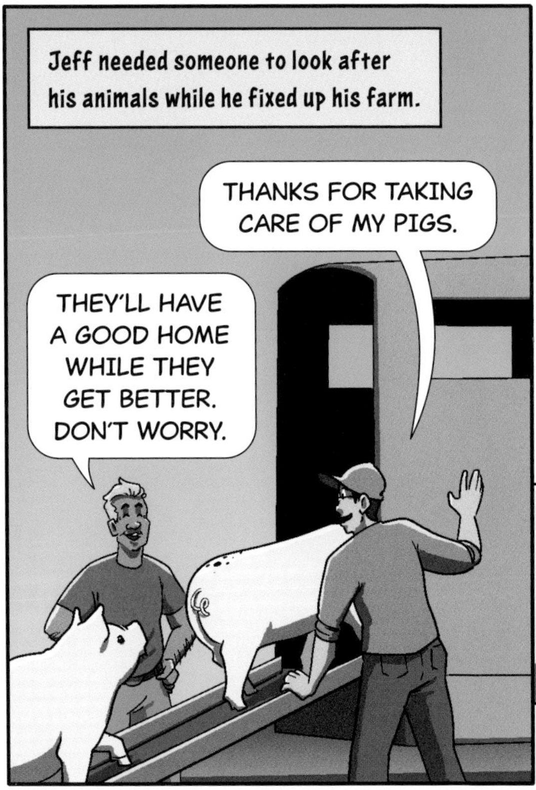
Jeff needed someone to look after his animals while he fixed up his farm.
THANKS FOR TAKING CARE OF MY PIGS.
THEY'LL HAVE A GOOD HOME WHILE THEY GET BETTER. DON'T WORRY.

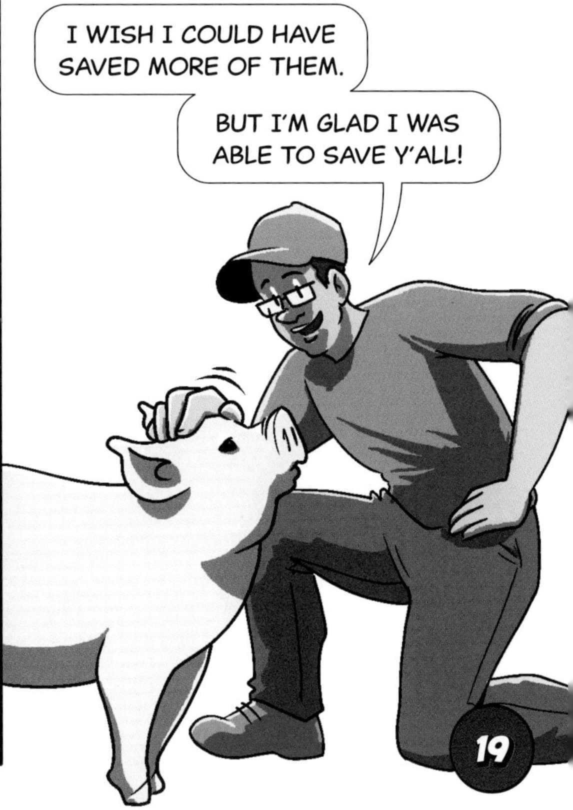
I WISH I COULD HAVE SAVED MORE OF THEM.
BUT I'M GLAD I WAS ABLE TO SAVE Y'ALL!

Jeff arranged for most of his animals to be taken to a **sanctuary** farm that cares for animals.

FARM SANCTUARY
Watkins Glen
New York

Workers used special tools called hog boards when the pigs arrived.

These helped move the injured pigs into their new homes safely.

Veterinarians checked out all the pigs at the sanctuary. The pigs got the care they needed!

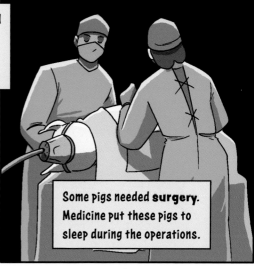

Some pigs needed **surgery**. Medicine put these pigs to sleep during the operations.

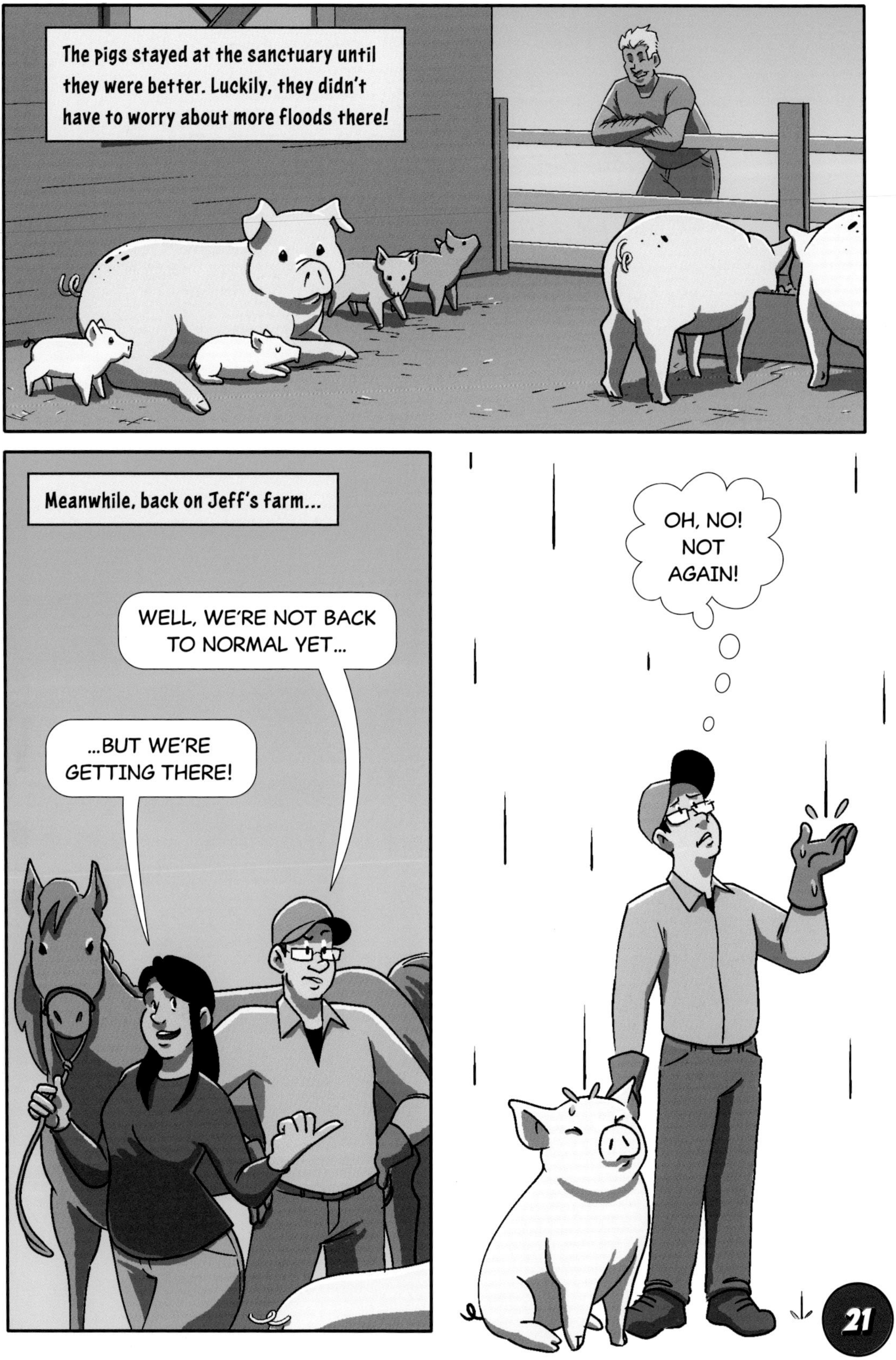
The pigs stayed at the sanctuary until they were better. Luckily, they didn't have to worry about more floods there!
Meanwhile, back on Jeff's farm...
WELL, WE'RE NOT BACK TO NORMAL YET...
...BUT WE'RE GETTING THERE!
OH, NO! NOT AGAIN!

OTHER FAMOUS FLOODS AND RESCUES

MIDWEST UNITED STATES, 2019

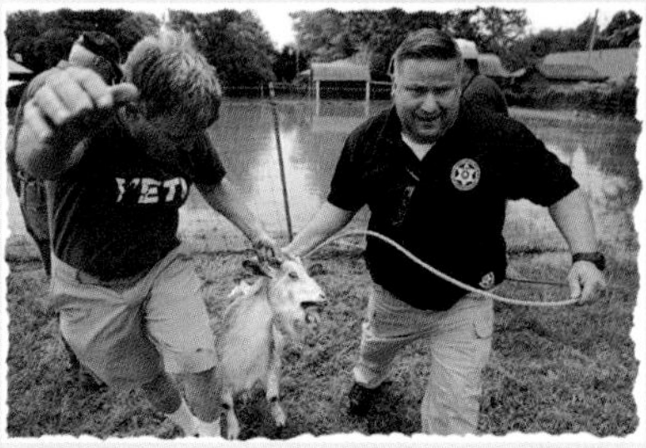
VET

In 2019, a series of rainstorms triggered flooding and broke dams across a wide area in the midwestern United States. There were floods in more than a dozen states from January to June. In Iowa, rescuers used **airboats** to pick up donkeys, goats, and ponies stranded by the rising waters. Oklahoma rescuers rushed to save dozens of drenched dogs and cats. In one Nebraska town, a dozen horses had to be led through knee-deep water to safety.

BRAZIL, 2011

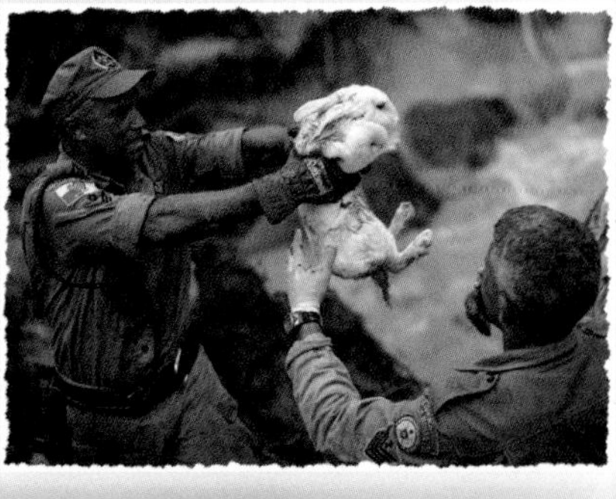

In 2011, violent rainstorms caused flooding and **mudslides** that buried entire Brazillian towns, killing nearly 1,000 people. When rescue workers reached some areas, they found many animals. The Animal Solidarity Campaign and their team of veterinarians, nurses, and volunteers treated and cared for sick and injured animals. Some animal rescue groups set up **shelters** for lost or abandoned animals so that pet owners could find them.

GLOSSARY

absorbed when liquid is taken in by a solid

airboats watercrafts that skim along the surface of water and are powered by a huge fan

banks the lands on the sides of a river

casts plaster coverings used to protect broken limbs

ease reduce or make less difficult

levee a wall-like structure made of earth, concrete, or other material that is built next to a body of water to prevent flooding

mudslides large amounts of mud or earth that move rapidly down a hill

overflow expand beyond what fits

sanctuary a safe place

shelters structures that provide protection

splints boards or stiff materials that hold broken limbs steady

stranded left behind

surgery a medical process in which doctors work inside a body

veterinarians doctors who take care of animals

INDEX

READ MORE

Black, Vanessa. *Floods (Disaster Zone)*. Minneapolis: Jump! Inc., 2017.

Hudak, Heather C. *Surviving the Flood: Hear My Story (Disaster Diaries)*. New York: Crabtree, 2020.

Waeschle, Amy. *Daring Flood Rescues (Edge Books. Rescued!)*. North Mankato, MN: Capstone Press, 2018.

LEARN MORE ONLINE

1. Go to **www.factsurfer.com**

2. Enter "**Water Everywhere**" into the search box.

3. Click on the cover of this book to see a list of websites.